D1238333

THE GENERAL ELECTION

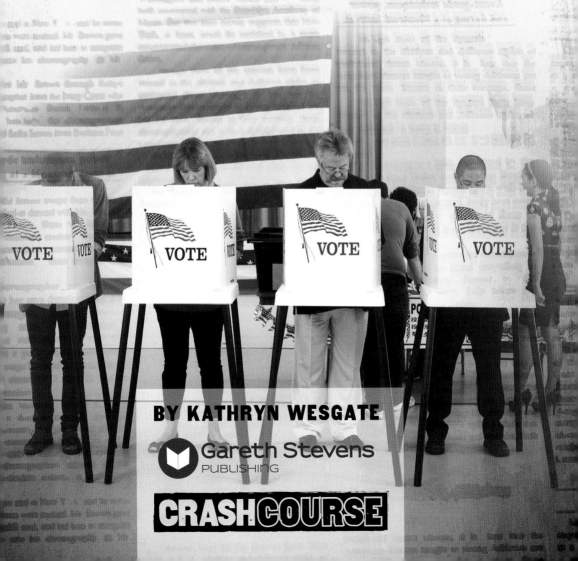

BY KATHRYN WESGATE

Gareth Stevens
PUBLISHING

CRASHCOURSE

Please visit our website, www.garethstevens.com. For a free color catalog of all our high-quality books, call toll free 1-800-542-2595 or fax 1-877-542-2596.

Library of Congress Cataloging-in-Publication Data
Names: Wesgate, Kathryn.
Title: The general election / Kathryn Wesgate.
Description: New York : Gareth Stevens Publishing, 2021. | Series: A look at U.S. elections | Includes glossary and index.
Identifiers: ISBN 9781538259504 (pbk.) | ISBN 9781538259528 (library bound) | ISBN 9781538259511(6 pack)
Subjects: LCSH: Presidents--United States--Election--Juvenile literature.
Classification: LCC JK524.W47 2021 | DDC 324.60973--dc23

First Edition

Published in 2021 by
Gareth Stevens Publishing
111 East 14th Street, Suite 349
New York, NY 10003

Editor: Kate Mikoley

Photo credits: Cover, pp. 1, 25 Hill Street Studios/DigitalVision/Getty Images; series art kzww/Shutterstock.com; series art (newspaper) MaryValery/Shutterstock.com; pp. 5, 29 Hero Images/Getty Images; p. 7 © iStock/outline205; p. 9 Jeff Greenberg/Universal Images Group/Getty Images; p. 11 Barbara Kalbfleisch/Shutterstock.com; p. 13 Courtesy of the Library of Congress; p. 15 Charles Ommanney/ Getty Images News/Getty Images; p. 17 Joseph Sohm/Shutterstock.com; p. 19 Lisa F. Young/Shutterstock.com; p. 21 Miljan Mladenovic/Shutterstock.com; p. 23 Rob Crandall/Shutterstock.com; p. 27 trekandshoot/Shutterstock.com; p. 30 (top left) JLMcAnally/Shutterstock.com; p. 30 (top right) Joseph Sohm/Shutterstock.com; p. 30 (bottom center) CL Shebley/Shutterstock.com.

Printed in the United States of America

Some of the images in this book illustrate individuals who are models. The depictions do not imply actual situations or events.

CPSIA compliance information: Batch #CS20GS: For further information contact Gareth Stevens, New York, New York at 1-800-542-2595.

Find us on 📘 📷

CONTENTS

Words in the glossary appear in **bold** type the first time they are used in the text.

ALL ABOUT ELECTIONS

An election is the act of picking someone for a government office. Elections let voters have a say in what happens where they live. There are different kinds of elections. The general election is the final election that decides who will fill an office.

MAKE THE GRADE

General elections let people pick leaders for their community, state, and country. Mayor, governor, and president are examples of positions filled through general elections.

5

WHO CAN VOTE?

Before you can vote in most general elections, you need to be registered, or signed up officially. The only state that doesn't require this is North Dakota. The way you register to vote is different from state to state.

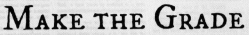

Voter Registration Application

form, review the General, Application, and Stat

This space fo

of America?

e election day?

either of these questions, do not complete form.

or rules regarding eligibility to register prior to age 18.)

Yes

Yes

No

No

First Name

Apt. or Lot #

City/Town

ame

City/To

7

To vote in a U.S. general election, you must be at least 18 years old. You must also be a U.S. **citizen**. States may have other rules too. For example, in some states, people found to have broken certain laws can't vote.

MAKE THE GRADE

In some states, you can register to vote as early as 16. You still can't vote until you're 18, but you'll be ready when your birthday comes around!

9

VOTING DAY

Federal general elections are held on the Tuesday after the first Monday in November. This started in 1845, when most voters were farmers and it took people a long time to get to and from their **polling places.**

MAKE THE GRADE
Before elections, **candidates** often campaign, or try to get people to vote for them.

In the 1800s it could take a whole day to get to your polling place! If the election were on the weekend or Monday, they'd need to travel on Sunday. Many people went to church on Sundays. Having the election on Tuesday made more sense. This practice continues to this day.

MAKE THE GRADE

Wednesdays wouldn't work either because it was market day—the day farmers went into town to sell their crops.

DEMOCRATS AND REPUBLICANS

In the United States, we have what's known as a two-party system. This means that, while there may be many **political parties**, most voters pick candidates in one of two major, or main, parties. In the United States, these are the Democrats and the Republicans.

Make the Grade

Before an election, candidates often take part in events called debates where they argue their thoughts on different subjects.

CHOOSING A CANDIDATE

Before a general election, there's often a primary. This is when people vote for who will run for a party in the general election. For example, in a Democratic presidential primary, voters choose who they want to run for the Democrats in the presidential general election.

MAKE THE GRADE

In a closed primary, voters must be part of the party they're voting for. An open primary is when any voter can vote for any candidate.

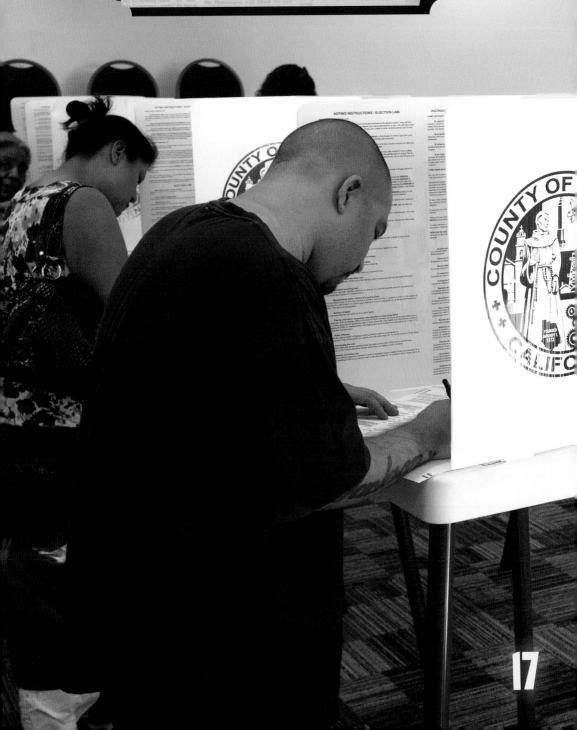

PICKING THE PRESIDENT

When you think of a general election, your first thought might be about the election that decides the president and vice president. These general elections happen every four years and are the ones that have the highest **voter turnout.**

Make the Grade

During presidential election years, most people pay attention to the candidates running for president and vice president, but there are other offices on these **ballots** too!

Elected presidents serve a **term** of four years and can serve up to two terms. In the presidential general election, voters choose who they want to be in this position. The result of their votes is called the popular vote.

ELECTING CONGRESS

General elections for members of Congress happen every two years, during even-numbered years. Sometimes these elections happen at the same time as the presidential election. When these elections take place between presidential elections they're called midterm elections.

MAKE THE GRADE

Congress is made up of two parts: the Senate and the House of Representatives. Senators are elected to six-year terms. Members of the House of Representatives serve two years.

Each state has two senators. The number of members a state has in the House of Representatives depends on its population. General elections for these leaders are important because their job is to look out for the interests of a state or **congressional district**.

MAKE THE GRADE

Elections for Congress are decided by the popular vote, not by electoral votes.

25

MORE ELECTIONS

Depending on where you live, general elections for state or local leaders may take place at different times of the year. They can also happen in different years than the elections for Congress or president. State general elections fill roles such as governor and state **legislature**.

Make the Grade

Local general elections decide who will fill official positions in a community. In cities, these people often work in a building called city hall.

CITY HALL

USE YOUR VOICE

General elections give citizens a chance to have a voice in their government. It's important to remember that these elections happen more than just every four years. Start learning about your leaders and government now and you'll be prepared to vote when you turn 18!

MAKE THE GRADE

You may be too young to vote now, but you can tell older family members how important it is to take part in general elections!

WAYS TO VOTE

Going to the polls isn't the only way
to vote. Here are a few other ways
people vote in general elections:

EARLY VOTING

Most states have set periods of
time people can vote in person
before Election Day.

ELECTRONIC VOTING

Some states let some voters who
live overseas vote online, either
on a special website or by email.

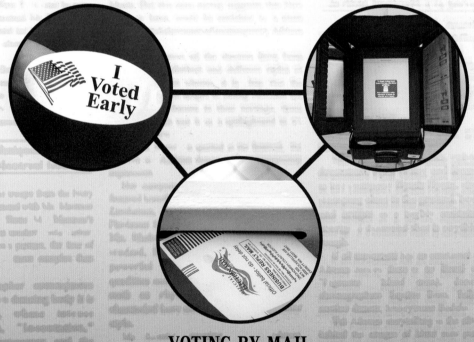

VOTING BY MAIL

If a voter can't make it to their
polling place on Election Day,
they may be able to get a ballot
early and mail it in.

GLOSSARY

ballot: a sheet of paper listing candidates' names and used for voting

candidate: a person who is running for office

citizen: someone who lives in a country legally and has certain rights

congressional district: the area in a state from which a member of the House of Representatives is elected

elector: a member of the Electoral College, a group of people chosen from each U.S. state who elect the president and vice president of the country based on the votes of the people in their state

federal: having to do with the national government

legislature: a lawmaking body

political party: a group of people with similar beliefs and ideas about government who work to have their members elected to government positions

polling place: a building where someone goes to vote that's decided by their address

population: the number of people living in a place

term: the length of time a person holds a government or official office

voter turnout: the percentage of those who can vote who actually vote in an election

FOR MORE INFORMATION

BOOKS

Conley, Kate. *Voting and Elections*. Minneapolis, MN: Core Library, an imprint of ABDO Publishing, 2017.

Martin, Bobi. *What Are Elections?* New York, NY: Britannica Educational Publishing in association with Rosen Educational Services, 2016.

WEBSITES

Presidential Election Process
www.usa.gov/election
Watch a video and view an infographic to see how people become president.

US Government: Two-Party System
www.ducksters.com/history/us_government/two-party_system.php
Learn more about the United States' two-party system and general election here.

Publisher's note to educators and parents: Our editors have carefully reviewed these websites to ensure that they are suitable for students. Many websites change frequently, however, and we cannot guarantee that a site's future contents will continue to meet our high standards of quality and educational value. Be advised that students should be closely supervised whenever they access the Internet.

INDEX